THIS JOURNAL
Belongs To:

_____

CAMPING *Adventures*

COLOR IN THE DATES WHEN YOU WENT CAMPING

JANUARY

S	M	T	W	T	F	S
		1	2	3	4	5
6	7	8	9	10	11	12
13	14	15	16	17	18	19
20	21	22	23	24	25	26
27	28	29	30	31		

FEBRUARY

S	M	T	W	T	F	S
					1	2
3	4	5	6	7	8	9
10	11	12	13	14	15	16
17	18	19	20	21	22	23
24	25	26	27	28		

MARCH

S	M	T	W	T	F	S
					1	2
3	4	5	6	7	8	9
10	11	12	13	14	15	16
17	18	19	20	21	22	23
24	25	26	27	28	29	30
31						

APRIL

S	M	T	W	T	F	S
	1	2	3	4	5	6
7	8	9	10	11	12	13
14	15	16	17	18	19	20
21	22	23	24	25	26	27
28	29	30				

MAY

S	M	T	W	T	F	S
			1	2	3	4
5	6	7	8	9	10	11
12	13	14	15	16	17	18
19	20	21	22	23	24	25
26	27	28	29	30	31	

JUNE

S	M	T	W	T	F	S
						1
2	3	4	5	6	7	8
9	10	11	12	13	14	15
16	17	18	19	20	21	22
23	24	25	26	27	28	29
30						

JULY

S	M	T	W	T	F	S
	1	2	3	4	5	6
7	8	9	10	11	12	13
14	15	16	17	18	19	20
21	22	23	24	25	26	27
28	29	30	31			

AUGUST

S	M	T	W	T	F	S
				1	2	3
4	5	6	7	8	9	10
11	12	13	14	15	16	17
18	19	20	21	22	23	24
25	26	27	28	29	30	31

SEPTEMBER

S	M	T	W	T	F	S
1	2	3	4	5	6	7
8	9	10	11	12	13	14
15	16	17	18	19	20	21
22	23	24	25	26	27	28
29	30					

OCTOBER

S	M	T	W	T	F	S
		1	2	3	4	5
6	7	8	9	10	11	12
13	14	15	16	17	18	19
20	21	22	23	24	25	26
27	28	29	30	31		

NOVEMBER

S	M	T	W	T	F	S
					1	2
3	4	5	6	7	8	9
10	11	12	13	14	15	16
17	18	19	20	21	22	23
24	25	26	27	28	29	30

DECEMBER

S	M	T	W	T	F	S
1	2	3	4	5	6	7
8	9	10	11	12	13	14
15	16	17	18	19	20	21
22	23	24	25	26	27	28
29	30	31				

CAMPING TRACKER
Where I've Been

CAMPGROUND	LOCATION	DATE

CAMPING RESERVATION

CAMPGROUND PHONE #	RESERVATION DETAILS
CONTACT PERSON	
CAMPGROUND ADDRESS	ACTIVITIES
RESTAURANTS & AMENITIES	NOTES

SITE #	NIGHTLY RATE	CHECK IN	CHECK OUT

CAMPGROUND
Amenities

- ○ WATER
- ○ ELECTRIC
- ○ SEWER
- ○ WIFI
- ○ CABLE TV
- ○ PETS ALLOWED
- ○ FIRE PIT
- ○ SHOWERS
- ○ TENTS PERMITTED
- ○ VISITOR PARKING
- ○ LAUNDRY SERVICES
- ○ BBQ AREA
- ○ SWIMMING
- ○ ACCESS TO BEACH / LAKE
- ○ BOAT LAUNCH
- ○ FISHING

- ○ POOL
- ○ HOT TUB
- ○ ACTIVITY CENTER
- ○ NATURE TRAILS / HIKING
- ○ PLAYGROUND
- ○ BIKING / TRAILS
- ○ GOLF COURSE
- ○ KIDS CENTER
- ○ FIREWORKS
- ○ BINGO
- ○ VOLLEYBALL
- ○ TENNIS COURTS
- ○ GARBAGE DISPOSAL
- ○ CONVENIENCE STORE
- ○ FIREWOOD/KINDLE
- ○ PICNIC TABLES

CAMPING *Shopping List*

FAMILY CAMPING *Checklist*

IMPORTANT GEAR

- ☐ Tent
- ☐ Backpack
- ☐ Tarp
- ☐ BBQ
- ☐ Sleeping Bag
- ☐ Camping Chairs
- ☐ _____
- ☐ _____
- ☐ _____
- ☐ _____
- ☐ _____

FOOD SUPPLIES

- ☐ Meals
- ☐ Snacks
- ☐ Water & Drinks
- ☐ Cook Set / Pots & Utensils & Dishes
- ☐ Condiments
- ☐ _____
- ☐ _____
- ☐ _____
- ☐ _____
- ☐ _____

CLOTHING

- ☐ Gloves & Hat
- ☐ Hats / Visors
- ☐ Socks & Underwear
- ☐ T-shirts & Sweaters
- ☐ Jacket / Raincoat
- ☐ Hiking Boots
- ☐ _____
- ☐ _____
- ☐ _____
- ☐ _____

TOOLS & SUPPLIES

- ☐ Lighter & Flashlights
- ☐ Firewood & Fire Starter
- ☐ Batteries
- ☐ Knife or Multi-Tool
- ☐ Compass
- ☐ _____
- ☐ _____
- ☐ _____
- ☐ _____
- ☐ _____

MISC ITEMS

- ☐ Garbage Bags
- ☐ Sunscreen
- ☐ Bug Spray/ Repellent
- ☐ Towels
- ☐ Water Bottle
- ☐ Toilet Paper
- ☐ _____
- ☐ _____
- ☐ _____
- ☐ _____

OTHER

- ☐ _____
- ☐ _____
- ☐ _____
- ☐ _____
- ☐ _____
- ☐ _____
- ☐ _____
- ☐ _____
- ☐ _____
- ☐ _____

FAMILY CAMPING Checklist

IMPORTANT GEAR
- [ ]
- [ ]
- [ ]
- [ ]
- [ ]
- [ ]
- [ ]
- [ ]
- [ ]
- [ ]
- [ ]

FOOD SUPPLIES
- [ ]
- [ ]
- [ ]
- [ ]
- [ ]
- [ ]
- [ ]
- [ ]
- [ ]
- [ ]
- [ ]

CLOTHING
- [ ]
- [ ]
- [ ]
- [ ]
- [ ]
- [ ]
- [ ]
- [ ]
- [ ]
- [ ]
- [ ]

TOOLS & SUPPLIES
- [ ]
- [ ]
- [ ]
- [ ]
- [ ]
- [ ]
- [ ]
- [ ]
- [ ]
- [ ]
- [ ]

MISC ITEMS
- [ ]
- [ ]
- [ ]
- [ ]
- [ ]
- [ ]
- [ ]
- [ ]
- [ ]
- [ ]
- [ ]

OTHER
- [ ]
- [ ]
- [ ]
- [ ]
- [ ]
- [ ]
- [ ]
- [ ]
- [ ]
- [ ]
- [ ]

CAMPING SUPPLIES

CAMPING *Checklist*

Shelter
- [ ] TENT / CAMPER
- [ ] SLEEPING BLANKET
- [ ] PILLOWS
- [ ] TARP / COVERING

Comfort
- [ ] SLEEPING BAGS
- [ ] SHEETS & PILLOWS
- [ ] AIR MATTRESS
- [ ] AIR PUMP

Clothing
- [ ] HIKING BOOTS
- [ ] SWEATERS
- [ ] RAIN JACKET
- [ ] WARM SOCKS
- [ ] T-SHIRTS
- [ ] WARM COAT
- [ ] SUN VISOR / HAT
- [ ] BATHING SUIT
- [ ] PYJAMAS

Food
- [ ] FOOD / SUPPLIES
- [ ] CONDIMENTS
- [ ] COOKWARE/POTS
- [ ] TABLE CLOTH
- [ ] PLATES & CUPS
- [ ] UTENSILS
- [ ] PAPER TOWEL
- [ ] POT HOLDERS
- [ ] DISH SOAP
- [ ] CUTLERY

Personal
- [ ] SOAP
- [ ] SHAMPOO
- [ ] TOWELS
- [ ] TOOTHPASTE
- [ ] HAIR BRUSH
- [ ] SUNSCREEN
- [ ] DEODORANT
- [ ] HAND SANITIZER
- [ ] RAZORS

Essentials
- [ ] MEDICATION
- [ ] FIRST AID KIT
- [ ] TOILET PAPER
- [ ] LIP BALM
- [ ] TISSUES
- [ ] MIRROR
- [ ] HAIR CLIPS

Important
- [ ] BATTERIES
- [ ] CAMERA
- [ ] CHARGERS
- [ ] SUNGLASSES
- [ ] FLASHLIGHT
- [ ] BUG SPRAY
- [ ] LANTERNS
- [ ] COMPASS
- [ ] BINOCULARS
- [ ] HIKING GEAR
- [ ] BACKPACK

CAMPING *Checklist*

Entertainment

- [ ] BOARD GAMES
- [ ] CARDS
- [ ] RADIO
- [ ] SPORTS GEAR

Cleaning

- [ ] BROOM / MOP
- [ ] CLEANING SUPPLIES
- [ ] CLEANING CLOTHS
- [ ] DISH TOWELS

Misc

- [ ] COFFEE POT
- [ ] FIRE KETTLE
- [ ] COOLER & ICE
- [ ] FOLDABLE TABLE
- [ ] CAMPING CHAIRS
- [ ] LIGHTER / FUEL
- [ ] FIREWOOD
- [ ] BBQ GRLL
- [ ] GARBAGE BAGS

Shopping List

- [ ]
- [ ]
- [ ]
- [ ]
- [ ]
- [ ]
- [ ]
- [ ]
- [ ]
- [ ]
- [ ]
- [ ]
- [ ]
- [ ]
- [ ]
- [ ]
- [ ]
- [ ]
- [ ]
- [ ]
- [ ]

CAMPING MEAL
Planner

MONDAY	TUESDAY

WEDNESDAY	THURSDAY

FRIDAY	SATURDAY

SUNDAY	SNACK IDEAS

CAMPING *Activities*

Monday

Tuesday

Wednesday

Thursday

Friday

Saturday

Sunday

MY CAMPING *Journal*

DATE:

WHAT I DID TODAY

HIGHLIGHT OF THE DAY

CAMPING *Memories*

DATE & CAMPSITE

WHAT WE DID

HIGHLIGHT OF THE TRIP

FISHING EXPEDITION
What I've Caught

LAKE / AREA	TYPE OF FISH	WEIGHT

FAMILY CAMPING
Adventures

CAMPGROUND

DATE

ACTIVITIES

HIGHLIGHT OF THE TRIP

FAVORITE MEMORY

HIKING CHECKLIST

CLOTHING

- ☐ HIKING BOOTS
- ☐ WOOL SOCKS
- ☐ BASE LAYERS
- ☐ SHORT SLEEVED SHIRT
- ☐ LONG SLEEVED SHIRT
- ☐ INSULATED MIDLAYER
- ☐ SUN HAT / VISOR
- ☐ BANDANA
- ☐ RAINWEAR
- ☐ WATCH

EQUIPMENT

- ☐ MAP
- ☐ COMPASS
- ☐ FLASHLIGHT
- ☐ HEAD LAMP
- ☐ LIGHTER / MATCHES
- ☐ KNIFE / MULTI-TOOL
- ☐ CELL PHONE
- ☐ POUCH
- ☐ MOLESKIN
- ☐ TREKKING POLES

FOOD & SUPPLIES

- ☐ MEALS & SNACKS
- ☐ WATER BOTTLE
- ☐ WATER TREATMENT
- ☐ COOKING POT
- ☐ COOKSTOVE/FUEL
- ☐ EATING UTENSILS
- ☐ BOWL/MUG/PLATE
- ☐ GARBAGE BAGS
- ☐ ROPE
- ☐ FOLDABLE BUCKET

CAMPING GEAR

- ☐ TENT
- ☐ SLEEPING BAG
- ☐ SLEEPING PAD
- ☐ TOILET PAPER
- ☐ BACKPACK
- ☐ DUCT TAPE
- ☐ FOLDING SAW
- ☐ POT LIFTER
- ☐ CAMP SHOES
- ☐ BEAR BANGER

MISC.

- ☐ INSECT REPELLENT
- ☐ LIP BALM
- ☐ FACE PROTECTOR
- ☐ EXTRA GLOVES
- ☐ DEODORANT
- ☐ HEADPHONES
- ☐ BATTERIES
- ☐ CHARGER
- ☐ DECK OF CARDS
- ☐ GPS

OTHER

- ☐ _____
- ☐ _____
- ☐ _____
- ☐ _____
- ☐ _____
- ☐ _____
- ☐ _____
- ☐ _____
- ☐ _____
- ☐ _____

HIKING JOURNAL

TRAIL	ELEVATION GAIN	LOSS
LOCATION		

DISTANCE	DURATION	START TIME	END TIME

TRAIL TYPE	DIFFICULTY	WEATHER

IMPORTANT TRAIL DETAILS	NOTES
TRAIL SURFACE / EXPOSURE	

CAMPING *Adventures*

COLOR IN THE DATES WHEN YOU WENT CAMPING

JANUARY

S	M	T	W	T	F	S
	1	2	3	4	5	
6	7	8	9	10	11	12
13	14	15	16	17	18	19
20	21	22	23	24	25	26
27	28	29	30	31		

FEBRUARY

S	M	T	W	T	F	S
					1	2
3	4	5	6	7	8	9
10	11	12	13	14	15	16
17	18	19	20	21	22	23
24	25	26	27	28		

MARCH

S	M	T	W	T	F	S
					1	2
3	4	5	6	7	8	9
10	11	12	13	14	15	16
17	18	19	20	21	22	23
24	25	26	27	28	29	30
31						

APRIL

S	M	T	W	T	F	S
	1	2	3	4	5	6
7	8	9	10	11	12	13
14	15	16	17	18	19	20
21	22	23	24	25	26	27
28	29	30				

MAY

S	M	T	W	T	F	S
			1	2	3	4
5	6	7	8	9	10	11
12	13	14	15	16	17	18
19	20	21	22	23	24	25
26	27	28	29	30	31	

JUNE

S	M	T	W	T	F	S
						1
2	3	4	5	6	7	8
9	10	11	12	13	14	15
16	17	18	19	20	21	22
23	24	25	26	27	28	29
30						

JULY

S	M	T	W	T	F	S
	1	2	3	4	5	6
7	8	9	10	11	12	13
14	15	16	17	18	19	20
21	22	23	24	25	26	27
28	29	30	31			

AUGUST

S	M	T	W	T	F	S
				1	2	3
4	5	6	7	8	9	10
11	12	13	14	15	16	17
18	19	20	21	22	23	24
25	26	27	28	29	30	31

SEPTEMBER

S	M	T	W	T	F	S
1	2	3	4	5	6	7
8	9	10	11	12	13	14
15	16	17	18	19	20	21
22	23	24	25	26	27	28
29	30					

OCTOBER

S	M	T	W	T	F	S
		1	2	3	4	5
6	7	8	9	10	11	12
13	14	15	16	17	18	19
20	21	22	23	24	25	26
27	28	29	30	31		

NOVEMBER

S	M	T	W	T	F	S
					1	2
3	4	5	6	7	8	9
10	11	12	13	14	15	16
17	18	19	20	21	22	23
24	25	26	27	28	29	30

DECEMBER

S	M	T	W	T	F	S
1	2	3	4	5	6	7
8	9	10	11	12	13	14
15	16	17	18	19	20	21
22	23	24	25	26	27	28
29	30	31				

CAMPING TRACKER
Where I've Been

CAMPGROUND	LOCATION	DATE

CAMPING RESERVATION

CAMPGROUND PHONE #	RESERVATION DETAILS
CONTACT PERSON	
CAMPGROUND ADDRESS	ACTIVITIES
RESTAURANTS & AMENITIES	NOTES

SITE #	NIGHTLY RATE	CHECK IN	CHECK OUT

CAMPGROUND
Amenities

- ○ WATER
- ○ ELECTRIC
- ○ SEWER
- ○ WIFI
- ○ CABLE TV
- ○ PETS ALLOWED
- ○ FIRE PIT
- ○ SHOWERS
- ○ TENTS PERMITTED
- ○ VISITOR PARKING
- ○ LAUNDRY SERVICES
- ○ BBQ AREA
- ○ SWIMMING
- ○ ACCESS TO BEACH / LAKE
- ○ BOAT LAUNCH
- ○ FISHING
- ○
- ○
- ○

- ○ POOL
- ○ HOT TUB
- ○ ACTIVITY CENTER
- ○ NATURE TRAILS / HIKING
- ○ PLAYGROUND
- ○ BIKING / TRAILS
- ○ GOLF COURSE
- ○ KIDS CENTER
- ○ FIREWORKS
- ○ BINGO
- ○ VOLLEYBALL
- ○ TENNIS COURTS
- ○ GARBAGE DISPOSAL
- ○ CONVENIENCE STORE
- ○ FIREWOOD/KINDLE
- ○ PICNIC TABLES
- ○
- ○
- ○

CAMPING *Shopping List*

CAMPING RESERVATION

CAMPGROUND PHONE #	RESERVATION DETAILS
CONTACT PERSON	
CAMPGROUND ADDRESS	ACTIVITIES
RESTAURANTS & AMENITIES	NOTES

SITE #	NIGHTLY RATE	CHECK IN	CHECK OUT

CAMPGROUND
Amenities

- ○ WATER
- ○ ELECTRIC
- ○ SEWER
- ○ WIFI
- ○ CABLE TV
- ○ PETS ALLOWED
- ○ FIRE PIT
- ○ SHOWERS
- ○ TENTS PERMITTED
- ○ VISITOR PARKING
- ○ LAUNDRY SERVICES
- ○ BBQ AREA
- ○ SWIMMING
- ○ ACCESS TO BEACH / LAKE
- ○ BOAT LAUNCH
- ○ FISHING
- ○
- ○
- ○

- ○ POOL
- ○ HOT TUB
- ○ ACTIVITY CENTER
- ○ NATURE TRAILS / HIKING
- ○ PLAYGROUND
- ○ BIKING / TRAILS
- ○ GOLF COURSE
- ○ KIDS CENTER
- ○ FIREWORKS
- ○ BINGO
- ○ VOLLEYBALL
- ○ TENNIS COURTS
- ○ GARBAGE DISPOSAL
- ○ CONVENIENCE STORE
- ○ FIREWOOD/KINDLE
- ○ PICNIC TABLES

CAMPING *Shopping List*

FAMILY CAMPING *Checklist*

IMPORTANT GEAR

- ☐ Tent
- ☐ Backpack
- ☐ Tarp
- ☐ BBQ
- ☐ Sleeping Bag
- ☐ Camping Chairs
- ☐ _____
- ☐ _____
- ☐ _____
- ☐ _____
- ☐ _____

FOOD SUPPLIES

- ☐ Meals
- ☐ Snacks
- ☐ Water & Drinks
- ☐ Cook Set / Pots &
- ☐ Utensils & Dishes
- ☐ Condiments
- ☐ _____
- ☐ _____
- ☐ _____
- ☐ _____
- ☐ _____

CLOTHING

- ☐ Gloves & Hat
- ☐ Hats / Visors
- ☐ Socks & Underwear
- ☐ T-shirts & Sweaters
- ☐ Jacket / Raincoat
- ☐ Hiking Boots
- ☐ _____
- ☐ _____
- ☐ _____
- ☐ _____
- ☐ _____

TOOLS & SUPPLIES

- ☐ Lighter & Flashlights
- ☐ Firewood & Fire Starter
- ☐ Batteries
- ☐ Knife or Multi-Tool
- ☐ Compass
- ☐ _____
- ☐ _____
- ☐ _____
- ☐ _____
- ☐ _____

MISC ITEMS

- ☐ Garbage Bags
- ☐ Sunscreen
- ☐ Bug Spray/ Repellent
- ☐ Towels
- ☐ Water Bottle
- ☐ Toilet Paper
- ☐ _____
- ☐ _____
- ☐ _____
- ☐ _____

OTHER

- ☐ _____
- ☐ _____
- ☐ _____
- ☐ _____
- ☐ _____
- ☐ _____
- ☐ _____
- ☐ _____
- ☐ _____
- ☐ _____

FAMILY CAMPING *Checklist*

IMPORTANT GEAR
- [ ] _____
- [ ] _____
- [ ] _____
- [ ] _____
- [ ] _____
- [ ] _____
- [ ] _____
- [ ] _____
- [ ] _____
- [ ] _____
- [ ] _____

FOOD SUPPLIES
- [ ] _____
- [ ] _____
- [ ] _____
- [ ] _____
- [ ] _____
- [ ] _____
- [ ] _____
- [ ] _____
- [ ] _____
- [ ] _____
- [ ] _____

CLOTHING
- [ ] _____
- [ ] _____
- [ ] _____
- [ ] _____
- [ ] _____
- [ ] _____
- [ ] _____
- [ ] _____
- [ ] _____
- [ ] _____
- [ ] _____

TOOLS & SUPPLIES
- [ ] _____
- [ ] _____
- [ ] _____
- [ ] _____
- [ ] _____
- [ ] _____
- [ ] _____
- [ ] _____
- [ ] _____
- [ ] _____
- [ ] _____

MISC ITEMS
- [ ] _____
- [ ] _____
- [ ] _____
- [ ] _____
- [ ] _____
- [ ] _____
- [ ] _____
- [ ] _____
- [ ] _____
- [ ] _____
- [ ] _____

OTHER
- [ ] _____
- [ ] _____
- [ ] _____
- [ ] _____
- [ ] _____
- [ ] _____
- [ ] _____
- [ ] _____
- [ ] _____
- [ ] _____
- [ ] _____

CAMPING SUPPLIES

CAMPING Checklist

Shelter
- [ ] TENT / CAMPER
- [ ] SLEEPING BLANKET
- [ ] PILLOWS
- [ ] TARP / COVERING

Comfort
- [ ] SLEEPING BAGS
- [ ] SHEETS & PILLOWS
- [ ] AIR MATTRESS
- [ ] AIR PUMP

Clothing
- [ ] HIKING BOOTS
- [ ] SWEATERS
- [ ] RAIN JACKET
- [ ] WARM SOCKS
- [ ] T-SHIRTS
- [ ] WARM COAT
- [ ] SUN VISOR / HAT
- [ ] BATHING SUIT
- [ ] PYJAMAS

Food
- [ ] FOOD / SUPPLIES
- [ ] CONDIMENTS
- [ ] COOKWARE/POTS
- [ ] TABLE CLOTH
- [ ] PLATES & CUPS
- [ ] UTENSILS
- [ ] PAPER TOWEL
- [ ] POT HOLDERS
- [ ] DISH SOAP
- [ ] CUTLERY

Personal
- [ ] SOAP
- [ ] SHAMPOO
- [ ] TOWELS
- [ ] TOOTHPASTE
- [ ] HAIR BRUSH
- [ ] SUNSCREEN
- [ ] DEODORANT
- [ ] HAND SANITIZER
- [ ] RAZORS

Essentials
- [ ] MEDICATION
- [ ] FIRST AID KIT
- [ ] TOILET PAPER
- [ ] LIP BALM
- [ ] TISSUES
- [ ] MIRROR
- [ ] HAIR CLIPS

Important
- [ ] BATTERIES
- [ ] CAMERA
- [ ] CHARGERS
- [ ] SUNGLASSES
- [ ] FLASHLIGHT
- [ ] BUG SPRAY
- [ ] LANTERNS
- [ ] COMPASS
- [ ] BINOCULARS
- [ ] HIKING GEAR
- [ ] BACKPACK

CAMPING Checklist

Entertainment
- [ ] BOARD GAMES
- [ ] CARDS
- [ ] RADIO
- [ ] SPORTS GEAR

Cleaning
- [ ] BROOM / MOP
- [ ] CLEANING SUPPLIES
- [ ] CLEANING CLOTHS
- [ ] DISH TOWELS

Misc
- [ ] COFFEE POT
- [ ] FIRE KETTLE
- [ ] COOLER & ICE
- [ ] FOLDABLE TABLE
- [ ] CAMPING CHAIRS
- [ ] LIGHTER / FUEL
- [ ] FIREWOOD
- [ ] BBQ GRLL
- [ ] GARBAGE BAGS

Shopping List

CAMPING MEAL
Planner

MONDAY	TUESDAY

WEDNESDAY	THURSDAY

FRIDAY	SATURDAY

SUNDAY	SNACK IDEAS

CAMPING *Activities*

 *Monday*

 *Tuesday*

 *Wednesday*

 *Thursday*

 *Friday*

 *Saturday*

 *Sunday*

MY CAMPING *Journal*

DATE:

WHAT I DID TODAY

HIGHLIGHT OF THE DAY

CAMPING *Memories*

DATE & CAMPSITE

WHAT WE DID

HIGHLIGHT OF THE TRIP

FISHING EXPEDITION
What I've Caught

LAKE / AREA	TYPE OF FISH	WEIGHT

FAMILY CAMPING
Adventures

CAMPGROUND

DATE

ACTIVITIES

HIGHLIGHT OF THE TRIP

FAVORITE MEMORY

HIKING CHECKLIST

CLOTHING

- ☐ HIKING BOOTS
- ☐ WOOL SOCKS
- ☐ BASE LAYERS
- ☐ SHORT SLEEVED SHIRT
- ☐ LONG SLEEVED SHIRT
- ☐ INSULATED MIDLAYER
- ☐ SUN HAT / VISOR
- ☐ BANDANA
- ☐ RAINWEAR
- ☐ WATCH

EQUIPMENT

- ☐ MAP
- ☐ COMPASS
- ☐ FLASHLIGHT
- ☐ HEAD LAMP
- ☐ LIGHTER / MATCHES
- ☐ KNIFE / MULTI-TOOL
- ☐ CELL PHONE
- ☐ POUCH
- ☐ MOLESKIN
- ☐ TREKKING POLES

FOOD & SUPPLIES

- ☐ MEALS & SNACKS
- ☐ WATER BOTTLE
- ☐ WATER TREATMENT
- ☐ COOKING POT
- ☐ COOKSTOVE/FUEL
- ☐ EATING UTENSILS
- ☐ BOWL/MUG/PLATE
- ☐ GARBAGE BAGS
- ☐ ROPE
- ☐ FOLDABLE BUCKET

CAMPING GEAR

- ☐ TENT
- ☐ SLEEPING BAG
- ☐ SLEEPING PAD
- ☐ TOILET PAPER
- ☐ BACKPACK
- ☐ DUCT TAPE
- ☐ FOLDING SAW
- ☐ POT LIFTER
- ☐ CAMP SHOES
- ☐ BEAR BANGER

MISC.

- ☐ INSECT REPELLENT
- ☐ LIP BALM
- ☐ FACE PROTECTOR
- ☐ EXTRA GLOVES
- ☐ DEODORANT
- ☐ HEADPHONES
- ☐ BATTERIES
- ☐ CHARGER
- ☐ DECK OF CARDS
- ☐ GPS

OTHER

- ☐ _____
- ☐ _____
- ☐ _____
- ☐ _____
- ☐ _____
- ☐ _____
- ☐ _____
- ☐ _____
- ☐ _____
- ☐ _____

HIKING JOURNAL

TRAIL		ELEVATION GAIN	LOSS
LOCATION			
DISTANCE	DURATION	START TIME	END TIME
TRAIL TYPE	DIFFICULTY	WEATHER	
IMPORTANT TRAIL DETAILS		NOTES	
TRAIL SURFACE	EXPOSURE		

CAMPING *Adventures*

COLOR IN THE DATES WHEN YOU WENT CAMPING

JANUARY

S	M	T	W	T	F	S
		1	2	3	4	5
6	7	8	9	10	11	12
13	14	15	16	17	18	19
20	21	22	23	24	25	26
27	28	29	30	31		

FEBRUARY

S	M	T	W	T	F	S
					1	2
3	4	5	6	7	8	9
10	11	12	13	14	15	16
17	18	19	20	21	22	23
24	25	26	27	28		

MARCH

S	M	T	W	T	F	S
					1	2
3	4	5	6	7	8	9
10	11	12	13	14	15	16
17	18	19	20	21	22	23
24	25	26	27	28	29	30
31						

APRIL

S	M	T	W	T	F	S
	1	2	3	4	5	6
7	8	9	10	11	12	13
14	15	16	17	18	19	20
21	22	23	24	25	26	27
28	29	30				

MAY

S	M	T	W	T	F	S
			1	2	3	4
5	6	7	8	9	10	11
12	13	14	15	16	17	18
19	20	21	22	23	24	25
26	27	28	29	30	31	

JUNE

S	M	T	W	T	F	S
						1
2	3	4	5	6	7	8
9	10	11	12	13	14	15
16	17	18	19	20	21	22
23	24	25	26	27	28	29
30						

JULY

S	M	T	W	T	F	S
	1	2	3	4	5	6
7	8	9	10	11	12	13
14	15	16	17	18	19	20
21	22	23	24	25	26	27
28	29	30	31			

AUGUST

S	M	T	W	T	F	S
				1	2	3
4	5	6	7	8	9	10
11	12	13	14	15	16	17
18	19	20	21	22	23	24
25	26	27	28	29	30	31

SEPTEMBER

S	M	T	W	T	F	S
1	2	3	4	5	6	7
8	9	10	11	12	13	14
15	16	17	18	19	20	21
22	23	24	25	26	27	28
29	30					

OCTOBER

S	M	T	W	T	F	S
		1	2	3	4	5
6	7	8	9	10	11	12
13	14	15	16	17	18	19
20	21	22	23	24	25	26
27	28	29	30	31		

NOVEMBER

S	M	T	W	T	F	S
					1	2
3	4	5	6	7	8	9
10	11	12	13	14	15	16
17	18	19	20	21	22	23
24	25	26	27	28	29	30

DECEMBER

S	M	T	W	T	F	S
1	2	3	4	5	6	7
8	9	10	11	12	13	14
15	16	17	18	19	20	21
22	23	24	25	26	27	28
29	30	31				

CAMPING TRACKER
Where I've Been

CAMPGROUND	LOCATION	DATE

CAMPING RESERVATION

CAMPGROUND PHONE #	RESERVATION DETAILS
CONTACT PERSON	
CAMPGROUND ADDRESS	ACTIVITIES
RESTAURANTS & AMENITIES	NOTES

SITE #	NIGHTLY RATE	CHECK IN	CHECK OUT

CAMPGROUND
Amenities

- ○ WATER
- ○ ELECTRIC
- ○ SEWER
- ○ WIFI
- ○ CABLE TV
- ○ PETS ALLOWED
- ○ FIRE PIT
- ○ SHOWERS
- ○ TENTS PERMITTED
- ○ VISITOR PARKING
- ○ LAUNDRY SERVICES
- ○ BBQ AREA
- ○ SWIMMING
- ○ ACCESS TO BEACH / LAKE
- ○ BOAT LAUNCH
- ○ FISHING
- ○
- ○
- ○

- ○ POOL
- ○ HOT TUB
- ○ ACTIVITY CENTER
- ○ NATURE TRAILS / HIKING
- ○ PLAYGROUND
- ○ BIKING / TRAILS
- ○ GOLF COURSE
- ○ KIDS CENTER
- ○ FIREWORKS
- ○ BINGO
- ○ VOLLEYBALL
- ○ TENNIS COURTS
- ○ GARBAGE DISPOSAL
- ○ CONVENIENCE STORE
- ○ FIREWOOD/KINDLE
- ○ PICNIC TABLES
- ○
- ○

CAMPING *Shopping List*

CAMPING RESERVATION

CAMPGROUND PHONE #	RESERVATION DETAILS
CONTACT PERSON	
CAMPGROUND ADDRESS	ACTIVITIES
RESTAURANTS & AMENITIES	NOTES

SITE #	NIGHTLY RATE	CHECK IN	CHECK OUT

CAMPGROUND
Amenities

- ○ WATER
- ○ ELECTRIC
- ○ SEWER
- ○ WIFI
- ○ CABLE TV
- ○ PETS ALLOWED
- ○ FIRE PIT
- ○ SHOWERS
- ○ TENTS PERMITTED
- ○ VISITOR PARKING
- ○ LAUNDRY SERVICES
- ○ BBQ AREA
- ○ SWIMMING
- ○ ACCESS TO BEACH / LAKE
- ○ BOAT LAUNCH
- ○ FISHING
- ○
- ○
- ○

- ○ POOL
- ○ HOT TUB
- ○ ACTIVITY CENTER
- ○ NATURE TRAILS / HIKING
- ○ PLAYGROUND
- ○ BIKING / TRAILS
- ○ GOLF COURSE
- ○ KIDS CENTER
- ○ FIREWORKS
- ○ BINGO
- ○ VOLLEYBALL
- ○ TENNIS COURTS
- ○ GARBAGE DISPOSAL
- ○ CONVENIENCE STORE
- ○ FIREWOOD/KINDLE
- ○ PICNIC TABLES
- ○
- ○
- ○

CAMPING *Shopping List*

FAMILY CAMPING *Checklist*

IMPORTANT GEAR

- ☐ Tent
- ☐ Backpack
- ☐ Tarp
- ☐ BBQ
- ☐ Sleeping Bag
- ☐ Camping Chairs
- ☐ _____
- ☐ _____
- ☐ _____
- ☐ _____
- ☐ _____

FOOD SUPPLIES

- ☐ Meals
- ☐ Snacks
- ☐ Water & Drinks
- ☐ Cook Set / Pots &
- ☐ Utensils & Dishes
- ☐ Condiments
- ☐ _____
- ☐ _____
- ☐ _____
- ☐ _____
- ☐ _____

CLOTHING

- ☐ Gloves & Hat
- ☐ Hats / Visors
- ☐ Socks & Underwear
- ☐ T-shirts & Sweaters
- ☐ Jacket / Raincoat
- ☐ Hiking Boots
- ☐ _____
- ☐ _____
- ☐ _____
- ☐ _____
- ☐ _____

TOOLS & SUPPLIES

- ☐ Lighter & Flashlights
- ☐ Firewood & Fire Starter
- ☐ Batteries
- ☐ Knife or Multi-Tool
- ☐ Compass
- ☐ _____
- ☐ _____
- ☐ _____
- ☐ _____
- ☐ _____

MISC ITEMS

- ☐ Garbage Bags
- ☐ Sunscreen
- ☐ Bug Spray/ Repellent
- ☐ Towels
- ☐ Water Bottle
- ☐ Toilet Paper
- ☐ _____
- ☐ _____
- ☐ _____
- ☐ _____

OTHER

- ☐ _____
- ☐ _____
- ☐ _____
- ☐ _____
- ☐ _____
- ☐ _____
- ☐ _____
- ☐ _____
- ☐ _____
- ☐ _____

FAMILY CAMPING *Checklist*

IMPORTANT GEAR
- [ ] _____
- [ ] _____
- [ ] _____
- [ ] _____
- [ ] _____
- [ ] _____
- [ ] _____
- [ ] _____
- [ ] _____
- [ ] _____
- [ ] _____

FOOD SUPPLIES
- [ ] _____
- [ ] _____
- [ ] _____
- [ ] _____
- [ ] _____
- [ ] _____
- [ ] _____
- [ ] _____
- [ ] _____
- [ ] _____
- [ ] _____

CLOTHING
- [ ] _____
- [ ] _____
- [ ] _____
- [ ] _____
- [ ] _____
- [ ] _____
- [ ] _____
- [ ] _____
- [ ] _____
- [ ] _____
- [ ] _____

TOOLS & SUPPLIES
- [ ] _____
- [ ] _____
- [ ] _____
- [ ] _____
- [ ] _____
- [ ] _____
- [ ] _____
- [ ] _____
- [ ] _____
- [ ] _____
- [ ] _____

MISC ITEMS
- [ ] _____
- [ ] _____
- [ ] _____
- [ ] _____
- [ ] _____
- [ ] _____
- [ ] _____
- [ ] _____
- [ ] _____
- [ ] _____
- [ ] _____

OTHER
- [ ] _____
- [ ] _____
- [ ] _____
- [ ] _____
- [ ] _____
- [ ] _____
- [ ] _____
- [ ] _____
- [ ] _____
- [ ] _____
- [ ] _____

CAMPING SUPPLIES

CAMPING Checklist

Shelter
- [ ] TENT / CAMPER
- [ ] SLEEPING BLANKET
- [ ] PILLOWS
- [ ] TARP / COVERING

Comfort
- [ ] SLEEPING BAGS
- [ ] SHEETS & PILLOWS
- [ ] AIR MATTRESS
- [ ] AIR PUMP

Clothing
- [ ] HIKING BOOTS
- [ ] SWEATERS
- [ ] RAIN JACKET
- [ ] WARM SOCKS
- [ ] T-SHIRTS
- [ ] WARM COAT
- [ ] SUN VISOR / HAT
- [ ] BATHING SUIT
- [ ] PYJAMAS

Food
- [ ] FOOD / SUPPLIES
- [ ] CONDIMENTS
- [ ] COOKWARE/POTS
- [ ] TABLE CLOTH
- [ ] PLATES & CUPS
- [ ] UTENSILS
- [ ] PAPER TOWEL
- [ ] POT HOLDERS
- [ ] DISH SOAP
- [ ] CUTLERY

Personal
- [ ] SOAP
- [ ] SHAMPOO
- [ ] TOWELS
- [ ] TOOTHPASTE
- [ ] HAIR BRUSH
- [ ] SUNSCREEN
- [ ] DEODORANT
- [ ] HAND SANITIZER
- [ ] RAZORS

Essentials
- [ ] MEDICATION
- [ ] FIRST AID KIT
- [ ] TOILET PAPER
- [ ] LIP BALM
- [ ] TISSUES
- [ ] MIRROR
- [ ] HAIR CLIPS

Important
- [ ] BATTERIES
- [ ] CAMERA
- [ ] CHARGERS
- [ ] SUNGLASSES
- [ ] FLASHLIGHT
- [ ] BUG SPRAY
- [ ] LANTERNS
- [ ] COMPASS
- [ ] BINOCULARS
- [ ] HIKING GEAR
- [ ] BACKPACK

CAMPING *Checklist*

Entertainment

- ☐ BOARD GAMES
- ☐ CARDS
- ☐ RADIO
- ☐ SPORTS GEAR

Cleaning

- ☐ BROOM / MOP
- ☐ CLEANING SUPPLIES
- ☐ CLEANING CLOTHS
- ☐ DISH TOWELS

Misc

- ☐ COFFEE POT
- ☐ FIRE KETTLE
- ☐ COOLER & ICE
- ☐ FOLDABLE TABLE
- ☐ CAMPING CHAIRS
- ☐ LIGHTER / FUEL
- ☐ FIREWOOD
- ☐ BBQ GRLL
- ☐ GARBAGE BAGS

Shopping List

CAMPING MEAL
Planner

MONDAY	TUESDAY

WEDNESDAY	THURSDAY

FRIDAY	SATURDAY

SUNDAY	SNACK IDEAS

CAMPING *Activities*

Monday

Tuesday

Wednesday

Thursday

Friday

Saturday

Sunday

MY CAMPING *Journal*

DATE:

WHAT I DID TODAY

HIGHLIGHT OF THE DAY

CAMPING *Memories*

DATE & CAMPSITE

WHAT WE DID

HIGHLIGHT OF THE TRIP

FISHING EXPEDITION
What I've Caught

LAKE / AREA	TYPE OF FISH	WEIGHT

FAMILY CAMPING
Adventures

CAMPGROUND   **DATE**

ACTIVITIES

HIGHLIGHT OF THE TRIP

FAVORITE MEMORY

HIKING CHECKLIST

CLOTHING

- ☐ HIKING BOOTS
- ☐ WOOL SOCKS
- ☐ BASE LAYERS
- ☐ SHORT SLEEVED SHIRT
- ☐ LONG SLEEVED SHIRT
- ☐ INSULATED MIDLAYER
- ☐ SUN HAT / VISOR
- ☐ BANDANA
- ☐ RAINWEAR
- ☐ WATCH

EQUIPMENT

- ☐ MAP
- ☐ COMPASS
- ☐ FLASHLIGHT
- ☐ HEAD LAMP
- ☐ LIGHTER / MATCHES
- ☐ KNIFE / MULTI-TOOL
- ☐ CELL PHONE
- ☐ POUCH
- ☐ MOLESKIN
- ☐ TREKKING POLES

FOOD & SUPPLIES

- ☐ MEALS & SNACKS
- ☐ WATER BOTTLE
- ☐ WATER TREATMENT
- ☐ COOKING POT
- ☐ COOKSTOVE/FUEL
- ☐ EATING UTENSILS
- ☐ BOWL/MUG/PLATE
- ☐ GARBAGE BAGS
- ☐ ROPE
- ☐ FOLDABLE BUCKET

CAMPING GEAR

- ☐ TENT
- ☐ SLEEPING BAG
- ☐ SLEEPING PAD
- ☐ TOILET PAPER
- ☐ BACKPACK
- ☐ DUCT TAPE
- ☐ FOLDING SAW
- ☐ POT LIFTER
- ☐ CAMP SHOES
- ☐ BEAR BANGER

MISC.

- ☐ INSECT REPELLENT
- ☐ LIP BALM
- ☐ FACE PROTECTOR
- ☐ EXTRA GLOVES
- ☐ DEODORANT
- ☐ HEADPHONES
- ☐ BATTERIES
- ☐ CHARGER
- ☐ DECK OF CARDS
- ☐ GPS

OTHER

- ☐ _____
- ☐ _____
- ☐ _____
- ☐ _____
- ☐ _____
- ☐ _____
- ☐ _____
- ☐ _____
- ☐ _____
- ☐ _____

HIKING JOURNAL

| TRAIL | ELEVATION GAIN | LOSS |
| LOCATION | | |

| DISTANCE | DURATION | START TIME | END TIME |

| TRAIL TYPE | DIFFICULTY | WEATHER |

| IMPORTANT TRAIL DETAILS | NOTES |

| TRAIL SURFACE | EXPOSURE | |

CAMPING Adventures

COLOR IN THE DATES WHEN YOU WENT CAMPING

JANUARY

S	M	T	W	T	F	S
		1	2	3	4	5
6	7	8	9	10	11	12
13	14	15	16	17	18	19
20	21	22	23	24	25	26
27	28	29	30	31		

FEBRUARY

S	M	T	W	T	F	S
					1	2
3	4	5	6	7	8	9
10	11	12	13	14	15	16
17	18	19	20	21	22	23
24	25	26	27	28		

MARCH

S	M	T	W	T	F	S
					1	2
3	4	5	6	7	8	9
10	11	12	13	14	15	16
17	18	19	20	21	22	23
24	25	26	27	28	29	30
31						

APRIL

S	M	T	W	T	F	S
	1	2	3	4	5	6
7	8	9	10	11	12	13
14	15	16	17	18	19	20
21	22	23	24	25	26	27
28	29	30				

MAY

S	M	T	W	T	F	S
			1	2	3	4
5	6	7	8	9	10	11
12	13	14	15	16	17	18
19	20	21	22	23	24	25
26	27	28	29	30	31	

JUNE

S	M	T	W	T	F	S
						1
2	3	4	5	6	7	8
9	10	11	12	13	14	15
16	17	18	19	20	21	22
23	24	25	26	27	28	29
30						

JULY

S	M	T	W	T	F	S
	1	2	3	4	5	6
7	8	9	10	11	12	13
14	15	16	17	18	19	20
21	22	23	24	25	26	27
28	29	30	31			

AUGUST

S	M	T	W	T	F	S
				1	2	3
4	5	6	7	8	9	10
11	12	13	14	15	16	17
18	19	20	21	22	23	24
25	26	27	28	29	30	31

SEPTEMBER

S	M	T	W	T	F	S
1	2	3	4	5	6	7
8	9	10	11	12	13	14
15	16	17	18	19	20	21
22	23	24	25	26	27	28
29	30					

OCTOBER

S	M	T	W	T	F	S
		1	2	3	4	5
6	7	8	9	10	11	12
13	14	15	16	17	18	19
20	21	22	23	24	25	26
27	28	29	30	31		

NOVEMBER

S	M	T	W	T	F	S
					1	2
3	4	5	6	7	8	9
10	11	12	13	14	15	16
17	18	19	20	21	22	23
24	25	26	27	28	29	30

DECEMBER

S	M	T	W	T	F	S
1	2	3	4	5	6	7
8	9	10	11	12	13	14
15	16	17	18	19	20	21
22	23	24	25	26	27	28
29	30	31				

CAMPING TRACKER
Where I've Been

CAMPGROUND	LOCATION	DATE

CAMPING RESERVATION

CAMPGROUND PHONE #	RESERVATION DETAILS
CONTACT PERSON	
CAMPGROUND ADDRESS	ACTIVITIES
RESTAURANTS & AMENITIES	NOTES

SITE #	NIGHTLY RATE	CHECK IN	CHECK OUT

CAMPGROUND
Amenities

- ○ WATER
- ○ ELECTRIC
- ○ SEWER
- ○ WIFI
- ○ CABLE TV
- ○ PETS ALLOWED
- ○ FIRE PIT
- ○ SHOWERS
- ○ TENTS PERMITTED
- ○ VISITOR PARKING
- ○ LAUNDRY SERVICES
- ○ BBQ AREA
- ○ SWIMMING
- ○ ACCESS TO BEACH / LAKE
- ○ BOAT LAUNCH
- ○ FISHING

- ○ POOL
- ○ HOT TUB
- ○ ACTIVITY CENTER
- ○ NATURE TRAILS / HIKING
- ○ PLAYGROUND
- ○ BIKING / TRAILS
- ○ GOLF COURSE
- ○ KIDS CENTER
- ○ FIREWORKS
- ○ BINGO
- ○ VOLLEYBALL
- ○ TENNIS COURTS
- ○ GARBAGE DISPOSAL
- ○ CONVENIENCE STORE
- ○ FIREWOOD/KINDLE
- ○ PICNIC TABLES

CAMPING *Shopping List*

CAMPING RESERVATION

CAMPGROUND PHONE #	RESERVATION DETAILS
CONTACT PERSON	
CAMPGROUND ADDRESS	ACTIVITIES
RESTAURANTS & AMENITIES	NOTES
SITE #	NIGHTLY RATE	CHECK IN	CHECK OUT

CAMPGROUND
Amenities

- ○ WATER
- ○ ELECTRIC
- ○ SEWER
- ○ WIFI
- ○ CABLE TV
- ○ PETS ALLOWED
- ○ FIRE PIT
- ○ SHOWERS
- ○ TENTS PERMITTED
- ○ VISITOR PARKING
- ○ LAUNDRY SERVICES
- ○ BBQ AREA
- ○ SWIMMING
- ○ ACCESS TO BEACH / LAKE
- ○ BOAT LAUNCH
- ○ FISHING

- ○ POOL
- ○ HOT TUB
- ○ ACTIVITY CENTER
- ○ NATURE TRAILS / HIKING
- ○ PLAYGROUND
- ○ BIKING / TRAILS
- ○ GOLF COURSE
- ○ KIDS CENTER
- ○ FIREWORKS
- ○ BINGO
- ○ VOLLEYBALL
- ○ TENNIS COURTS
- ○ GARBAGE DISPOSAL
- ○ CONVENIENCE STORE
- ○ FIREWOOD/KINDLE
- ○ PICNIC TABLES

CAMPING *Shopping List*

FAMILY CAMPING *Checklist*

IMPORTANT GEAR

- ☐ Tent
- ☐ Backpack
- ☐ Tarp
- ☐ BBQ
- ☐ Sleeping Bag
- ☐ Camping Chairs
- ☐ _____
- ☐ _____
- ☐ _____
- ☐ _____
- ☐ _____

FOOD SUPPLIES

- ☐ Meals
- ☐ Snacks
- ☐ Water & Drinks
- ☐ Cook Set / Pots &
- ☐ Utensils & Dishes
- ☐ Condiments
- ☐ _____
- ☐ _____
- ☐ _____
- ☐ _____
- ☐ _____

CLOTHING

- ☐ Gloves & Hat
- ☐ Hats / Visors
- ☐ Socks & Underwear
- ☐ T-shirts & Sweaters
- ☐ Jacket / Raincoat
- ☐ Hiking Boots
- ☐ _____
- ☐ _____
- ☐ _____
- ☐ _____
- ☐ _____

TOOLS & SUPPLIES

- ☐ Lighter & Flashlights
- ☐ Firewood & Fire Starter
- ☐ Batteries
- ☐ Knife or Multi-Tool
- ☐ Compass
- ☐ _____
- ☐ _____
- ☐ _____
- ☐ _____
- ☐ _____

MISC ITEMS

- ☐ Garbage Bags
- ☐ Sunscreen
- ☐ Bug Spray/ Repellent
- ☐ Towels
- ☐ Water Bottle
- ☐ Toilet Paper
- ☐ _____
- ☐ _____
- ☐ _____
- ☐ _____
- ☐ _____

OTHER

- ☐ _____
- ☐ _____
- ☐ _____
- ☐ _____
- ☐ _____
- ☐ _____
- ☐ _____
- ☐ _____
- ☐ _____
- ☐ _____
- ☐ _____

FAMILY CAMPING
Checklist

IMPORTANT GEAR

- [ ] _____
- [ ] _____
- [ ] _____
- [ ] _____
- [ ] _____
- [ ] _____
- [ ] _____
- [ ] _____
- [ ] _____
- [ ] _____

FOOD SUPPLIES

- [ ] _____
- [ ] _____
- [ ] _____
- [ ] _____
- [ ] _____
- [ ] _____
- [ ] _____
- [ ] _____
- [ ] _____
- [ ] _____

CLOTHING

- [ ] _____
- [ ] _____
- [ ] _____
- [ ] _____
- [ ] _____
- [ ] _____
- [ ] _____
- [ ] _____
- [ ] _____
- [ ] _____

TOOLS & SUPPLIES

- [ ] _____
- [ ] _____
- [ ] _____
- [ ] _____
- [ ] _____
- [ ] _____
- [ ] _____
- [ ] _____
- [ ] _____
- [ ] _____

MISC ITEMS

- [ ] _____
- [ ] _____
- [ ] _____
- [ ] _____
- [ ] _____
- [ ] _____
- [ ] _____
- [ ] _____
- [ ] _____
- [ ] _____

OTHER

- [ ] _____
- [ ] _____
- [ ] _____
- [ ] _____
- [ ] _____
- [ ] _____
- [ ] _____
- [ ] _____
- [ ] _____
- [ ] _____

CAMPING SUPPLIES

CAMPING *Checklist*

Shelter
- [ ] TENT / CAMPER
- [ ] SLEEPING BLANKET
- [ ] PILLOWS
- [ ] TARP / COVERING

Comfort
- [ ] SLEEPING BAGS
- [ ] SHEETS & PILLOWS
- [ ] AIR MATTRESS
- [ ] AIR PUMP

Clothing
- [ ] HIKING BOOTS
- [ ] SWEATERS
- [ ] RAIN JACKET
- [ ] WARM SOCKS
- [ ] T-SHIRTS
- [ ] WARM COAT
- [ ] SUN VISOR / HAT
- [ ] BATHING SUIT
- [ ] PYJAMAS

Food
- [ ] FOOD / SUPPLIES
- [ ] CONDIMENTS
- [ ] COOKWARE/POTS
- [ ] TABLE CLOTH
- [ ] PLATES & CUPS
- [ ] UTENSILS
- [ ] PAPER TOWEL
- [ ] POT HOLDERS
- [ ] DISH SOAP
- [ ] CUTLERY

Personal
- [ ] SOAP
- [ ] SHAMPOO
- [ ] TOWELS
- [ ] TOOTHPASTE
- [ ] HAIR BRUSH
- [ ] SUNSCREEN
- [ ] DEODORANT
- [ ] HAND SANITIZER
- [ ] RAZORS

Essentials
- [ ] MEDICATION
- [ ] FIRST AID KIT
- [ ] TOILET PAPER
- [ ] LIP BALM
- [ ] TISSUES
- [ ] MIRROR
- [ ] HAIR CLIPS

Important
- [ ] BATTERIES
- [ ] CAMERA
- [ ] CHARGERS
- [ ] SUNGLASSES
- [ ] FLASHLIGHT
- [ ] BUG SPRAY
- [ ] LANTERNS
- [ ] COMPASS
- [ ] BINOCULARS
- [ ] HIKING GEAR
- [ ] BACKPACK

CAMPING *Checklist*

Entertainment

- [ ] BOARD GAMES
- [ ] CARDS
- [ ] RADIO
- [ ] SPORTS GEAR

Cleaning

- [ ] BROOM / MOP
- [ ] CLEANING SUPPLIES
- [ ] CLEANING CLOTHS
- [ ] DISH TOWELS

Misc

- [ ] COFFEE POT
- [ ] FIRE KETTLE
- [ ] COOLER & ICE
- [ ] FOLDABLE TABLE
- [ ] CAMPING CHAIRS
- [ ] LIGHTER / FUEL
- [ ] FIREWOOD
- [ ] BBQ GRLL
- [ ] GARBAGE BAGS

Shopping List

CAMPING MEAL
Planner

MONDAY	TUESDAY

WEDNESDAY	THURSDAY

FRIDAY	SATURDAY

SUNDAY	SNACK IDEAS

CAMPING *Activities*

Monday

Tuesday

Wednesday

Thursday

Friday

Saturday

Sunday

MY CAMPING *Journal*

DATE:

WHAT I DID TODAY

HIGHLIGHT OF THE DAY

CAMPING *Memories*

DATE & CAMPSITE

WHAT WE DID

HIGHLIGHT OF THE TRIP

FISHING EXPEDITION
What I've Caught

LAKE / AREA	TYPE OF FISH	WEIGHT

FAMILY CAMPING
Adventures

CAMPGROUND

DATE

ACTIVITIES

HIGHLIGHT OF THE TRIP

FAVORITE MEMORY

HIKING CHECKLIST

CLOTHING

- ☐ HIKING BOOTS
- ☐ WOOL SOCKS
- ☐ BASE LAYERS
- ☐ SHORT SLEEVED SHIRT
- ☐ LONG SLEEVED SHIRT
- ☐ INSULATED MIDLAYER
- ☐ SUN HAT / VISOR
- ☐ BANDANA
- ☐ RAINWEAR
- ☐ WATCH

EQUIPMENT

- ☐ MAP
- ☐ COMPASS
- ☐ FLASHLIGHT
- ☐ HEAD LAMP
- ☐ LIGHTER / MATCHES
- ☐ KNIFE / MULTI-TOOL
- ☐ CELL PHONE
- ☐ POUCH
- ☐ MOLESKIN
- ☐ TREKKING POLES

FOOD & SUPPLIES

- ☐ MEALS & SNACKS
- ☐ WATER BOTTLE
- ☐ WATER TREATMENT
- ☐ COOKING POT
- ☐ COOKSTOVE/FUEL
- ☐ EATING UTENSILS
- ☐ BOWL/MUG/PLATE
- ☐ GARBAGE BAGS
- ☐ ROPE
- ☐ FOLDABLE BUCKET

CAMPING GEAR

- ☐ TENT
- ☐ SLEEPING BAG
- ☐ SLEEPING PAD
- ☐ TOILET PAPER
- ☐ BACKPACK
- ☐ DUCT TAPE
- ☐ FOLDING SAW
- ☐ POT LIFTER
- ☐ CAMP SHOES
- ☐ BEAR BANGER

MISC.

- ☐ INSECT REPELLENT
- ☐ LIP BALM
- ☐ FACE PROTECTOR
- ☐ EXTRA GLOVES
- ☐ DEODORANT
- ☐ HEADPHONES
- ☐ BATTERIES
- ☐ CHARGER
- ☐ DECK OF CARDS
- ☐ GPS

OTHER

- ☐ _____
- ☐ _____
- ☐ _____
- ☐ _____
- ☐ _____
- ☐ _____
- ☐ _____
- ☐ _____
- ☐ _____
- ☐ _____

HIKING JOURNAL

TRAIL		ELEVATION GAIN	LOSS
LOCATION			
DISTANCE	DURATION	START TIME	END TIME
TRAIL TYPE	DIFFICULTY	WEATHER	
IMPORTANT TRAIL DETAILS		NOTES	
TRAIL SURFACE	EXPOSURE		

CAMPING *Adventures*

COLOR IN THE DATES WHEN YOU WENT CAMPING

JANUARY
S	M	T	W	T	F	S
		1	2	3	4	5
6	7	8	9	10	11	12
13	14	15	16	17	18	19
20	21	22	23	24	25	26
27	28	29	30	31		

FEBRUARY
S	M	T	W	T	F	S
					1	2
3	4	5	6	7	8	9
10	11	12	13	14	15	16
17	18	19	20	21	22	23
24	25	26	27	28		

MARCH
S	M	T	W	T	F	S
					1	2
3	4	5	6	7	8	9
10	11	12	13	14	15	16
17	18	19	20	21	22	23
24	25	26	27	28	29	30
31						

APRIL
S	M	T	W	T	F	S
	1	2	3	4	5	6
7	8	9	10	11	12	13
14	15	16	17	18	19	20
21	22	23	24	25	26	27
28	29	30				

MAY
S	M	T	W	T	F	S
			1	2	3	4
5	6	7	8	9	10	11
12	13	14	15	16	17	18
19	20	21	22	23	24	25
26	27	28	29	30	31	

JUNE
S	M	T	W	T	F	S
						1
2	3	4	5	6	7	8
9	10	11	12	13	14	15
16	17	18	19	20	21	22
23	24	25	26	27	28	29
30						

JULY
S	M	T	W	T	F	S
	1	2	3	4	5	6
7	8	9	10	11	12	13
14	15	16	17	18	19	20
21	22	23	24	25	26	27
28	29	30	31			

AUGUST
S	M	T	W	T	F	S
				1	2	3
4	5	6	7	8	9	10
11	12	13	14	15	16	17
18	19	20	21	22	23	24
25	26	27	28	29	30	31

SEPTEMBER
S	M	T	W	T	F	S
1	2	3	4	5	6	7
8	9	10	11	12	13	14
15	16	17	18	19	20	21
22	23	24	25	26	27	28
29	30					

OCTOBER
S	M	T	W	T	F	S
		1	2	3	4	5
6	7	8	9	10	11	12
13	14	15	16	17	18	19
20	21	22	23	24	25	26
27	28	29	30	31		

NOVEMBER
S	M	T	W	T	F	S
					1	2
3	4	5	6	7	8	9
10	11	12	13	14	15	16
17	18	19	20	21	22	23
24	25	26	27	28	29	30

DECEMBER
S	M	T	W	T	F	S
1	2	3	4	5	6	7
8	9	10	11	12	13	14
15	16	17	18	19	20	21
22	23	24	25	26	27	28
29	30	31				

CAMPING TRACKER
Where I've Been

CAMPGROUND	LOCATION	DATE

CAMPING RESERVATION

CAMPGROUND PHONE #	RESERVATION DETAILS
CONTACT PERSON	
CAMPGROUND ADDRESS	ACTIVITIES
RESTAURANTS & AMENITIES	NOTES

SITE #	NIGHTLY RATE	CHECK IN	CHECK OUT

CAMPGROUND
Amenities

- ○ WATER
- ○ ELECTRIC
- ○ SEWER
- ○ WIFI
- ○ CABLE TV
- ○ PETS ALLOWED
- ○ FIRE PIT
- ○ SHOWERS
- ○ TENTS PERMITTED
- ○ VISITOR PARKING
- ○ LAUNDRY SERVICES
- ○ BBQ AREA
- ○ SWIMMING
- ○ ACCESS TO BEACH / LAKE
- ○ BOAT LAUNCH
- ○ FISHING

- ○ POOL
- ○ HOT TUB
- ○ ACTIVITY CENTER
- ○ NATURE TRAILS / HIKING
- ○ PLAYGROUND
- ○ BIKING / TRAILS
- ○ GOLF COURSE
- ○ KIDS CENTER
- ○ FIREWORKS
- ○ BINGO
- ○ VOLLEYBALL
- ○ TENNIS COURTS
- ○ GARBAGE DISPOSAL
- ○ CONVENIENCE STORE
- ○ FIREWOOD/KINDLE
- ○ PICNIC TABLES

CAMPING *Shopping List*

CAMPING RESERVATION

CAMPGROUND PHONE #	RESERVATION DETAILS
CONTACT PERSON	
CAMPGROUND ADDRESS	ACTIVITIES
RESTAURANTS & AMENITIES	NOTES

SITE #	NIGHTLY RATE	CHECK IN	CHECK OUT

CAMPGROUND
Amenities

- ○ WATER
- ○ ELECTRIC
- ○ SEWER
- ○ WIFI
- ○ CABLE TV
- ○ PETS ALLOWED
- ○ FIRE PIT
- ○ SHOWERS
- ○ TENTS PERMITTED
- ○ VISITOR PARKING
- ○ LAUNDRY SERVICES
- ○ BBQ AREA
- ○ SWIMMING
- ○ ACCESS TO BEACH / LAKE
- ○ BOAT LAUNCH
- ○ FISHING

- ○ POOL
- ○ HOT TUB
- ○ ACTIVITY CENTER
- ○ NATURE TRAILS / HIKING
- ○ PLAYGROUND
- ○ BIKING / TRAILS
- ○ GOLF COURSE
- ○ KIDS CENTER
- ○ FIREWORKS
- ○ BINGO
- ○ VOLLEYBALL
- ○ TENNIS COURTS
- ○ GARBAGE DISPOSAL
- ○ CONVENIENCE STORE
- ○ FIREWOOD/KINDLE
- ○ PICNIC TABLES

CAMPING Shopping List

FAMILY CAMPING *Checklist*

IMPORTANT GEAR

- ☐ Tent
- ☐ Backpack
- ☐ Tarp
- ☐ BBQ
- ☐ Sleeping Bag
- ☐ Camping Chairs
- ☐ _____
- ☐ _____
- ☐ _____
- ☐ _____
- ☐ _____

FOOD SUPPLIES

- ☐ Meals
- ☐ Snacks
- ☐ Water & Drinks
- ☐ Cook Set / Pots &
- ☐ Utensils & Dishes
- ☐ Condiments
- ☐ _____
- ☐ _____
- ☐ _____
- ☐ _____
- ☐ _____

CLOTHING

- ☐ Gloves & Hat
- ☐ Hats / Visors
- ☐ Socks & Underwear
- ☐ T-shirts & Sweaters
- ☐ Jacket / Raincoat
- ☐ Hiking Boots
- ☐ _____
- ☐ _____
- ☐ _____
- ☐ _____
- ☐ _____

TOOLS & SUPPLIES

- ☐ Lighter & Flashlights
- ☐ Firewood & Fire Starter
- ☐ Batteries
- ☐ Knife or Multi-Tool
- ☐ Compass
- ☐ _____
- ☐ _____
- ☐ _____
- ☐ _____
- ☐ _____

MISC ITEMS

- ☐ Garbage Bags
- ☐ Sunscreen
- ☐ Bug Spray/ Repellent
- ☐ Towels
- ☐ Water Bottle
- ☐ Toilet Paper
- ☐ _____
- ☐ _____
- ☐ _____
- ☐ _____

OTHER

- ☐ _____
- ☐ _____
- ☐ _____
- ☐ _____
- ☐ _____
- ☐ _____
- ☐ _____
- ☐ _____
- ☐ _____
- ☐ _____

FAMILY CAMPING *Checklist*

IMPORTANT GEAR
- [ ] _____
- [ ] _____
- [ ] _____
- [ ] _____
- [ ] _____
- [ ] _____
- [ ] _____
- [ ] _____
- [ ] _____
- [ ] _____
- [ ] _____

FOOD SUPPLIES
- [ ] _____
- [ ] _____
- [ ] _____
- [ ] _____
- [ ] _____
- [ ] _____
- [ ] _____
- [ ] _____
- [ ] _____
- [ ] _____
- [ ] _____

CLOTHING
- [ ] _____
- [ ] _____
- [ ] _____
- [ ] _____
- [ ] _____
- [ ] _____
- [ ] _____
- [ ] _____
- [ ] _____
- [ ] _____
- [ ] _____

TOOLS & SUPPLIES
- [ ] _____
- [ ] _____
- [ ] _____
- [ ] _____
- [ ] _____
- [ ] _____
- [ ] _____
- [ ] _____
- [ ] _____
- [ ] _____
- [ ] _____

MISC ITEMS
- [ ] _____
- [ ] _____
- [ ] _____
- [ ] _____
- [ ] _____
- [ ] _____
- [ ] _____
- [ ] _____
- [ ] _____
- [ ] _____
- [ ] _____

OTHER
- [ ] _____
- [ ] _____
- [ ] _____
- [ ] _____
- [ ] _____
- [ ] _____
- [ ] _____
- [ ] _____
- [ ] _____
- [ ] _____
- [ ] _____

CAMPING SUPPLIES

CAMPING *Checklist*

Shelter
- [ ] TENT / CAMPER
- [ ] SLEEPING BLANKET
- [ ] PILLOWS
- [ ] TARP / COVERING

Comfort
- [ ] SLEEPING BAGS
- [ ] SHEETS & PILLOWS
- [ ] AIR MATTRESS
- [ ] AIR PUMP

Clothing
- [ ] HIKING BOOTS
- [ ] SWEATERS
- [ ] RAIN JACKET
- [ ] WARM SOCKS
- [ ] T-SHIRTS
- [ ] WARM COAT
- [ ] SUN VISOR / HAT
- [ ] BATHING SUIT
- [ ] PYJAMAS

Food
- [ ] FOOD / SUPPLIES
- [ ] CONDIMENTS
- [ ] COOKWARE/POTS
- [ ] TABLE CLOTH
- [ ] PLATES & CUPS
- [ ] UTENSILS
- [ ] PAPER TOWEL
- [ ] POT HOLDERS
- [ ] DISH SOAP
- [ ] CUTLERY

Personal
- [ ] SOAP
- [ ] SHAMPOO
- [ ] TOWELS
- [ ] TOOTHPASTE
- [ ] HAIR BRUSH
- [ ] SUNSCREEN
- [ ] DEODORANT
- [ ] HAND SANITIZER
- [ ] RAZORS

Essentials
- [ ] MEDICATION
- [ ] FIRST AID KIT
- [ ] TOILET PAPER
- [ ] LIP BALM
- [ ] TISSUES
- [ ] MIRROR
- [ ] HAIR CLIPS

Important
- [ ] BATTERIES
- [ ] CAMERA
- [ ] CHARGERS
- [ ] SUNGLASSES
- [ ] FLASHLIGHT
- [ ] BUG SPRAY
- [ ] LANTERNS
- [ ] COMPASS
- [ ] BINOCULARS
- [ ] HIKING GEAR
- [ ] BACKPACK

CAMPING Checklist

Entertainment

- [ ] BOARD GAMES
- [ ] CARDS
- [ ] RADIO
- [ ] SPORTS GEAR

Cleaning

- [ ] BROOM / MOP
- [ ] CLEANING SUPPLIES
- [ ] CLEANING CLOTHS
- [ ] DISH TOWELS

Misc

- [ ] COFFEE POT
- [ ] FIRE KETTLE
- [ ] COOLER & ICE
- [ ] FOLDABLE TABLE
- [ ] CAMPING CHAIRS
- [ ] LIGHTER / FUEL
- [ ] FIREWOOD
- [ ] BBQ GRLL
- [ ] GARBAGE BAGS

Shopping List

- [ ]
- [ ]
- [ ]
- [ ]
- [ ]
- [ ]
- [ ]
- [ ]
- [ ]
- [ ]
- [ ]
- [ ]
- [ ]
- [ ]
- [ ]
- [ ]
- [ ]
- [ ]
- [ ]
- [ ]
- [ ]

CAMPING MEAL
Planner

MONDAY	TUESDAY

WEDNESDAY	THURSDAY

FRIDAY	SATURDAY

SUNDAY	SNACK IDEAS

CAMPING *Activities*

Monday

Tuesday

Wednesday

Thursday

Friday

Saturday

Sunday

MY CAMPING *Journal*

DATE:

WHAT I DID TODAY

HIGHLIGHT OF THE DAY

CAMPING *Memories*

DATE & CAMPSITE

WHAT WE DID

HIGHLIGHT OF THE TRIP

FISHING EXPEDITION
What I've Caught

LAKE / AREA	TYPE OF FISH	WEIGHT

FAMILY CAMPING
Adventures

CAMPGROUND   **DATE**

ACTIVITIES   **HIGHLIGHT OF THE TRIP**

FAVORITE MEMORY

HIKING CHECKLIST

CLOTHING

- ☐ HIKING BOOTS
- ☐ WOOL SOCKS
- ☐ BASE LAYERS
- ☐ SHORT SLEEVED SHIRT
- ☐ LONG SLEEVED SHIRT
- ☐ INSULATED MIDLAYER
- ☐ SUN HAT / VISOR
- ☐ BANDANA
- ☐ RAINWEAR
- ☐ WATCH

EQUIPMENT

- ☐ MAP
- ☐ COMPASS
- ☐ FLASHLIGHT
- ☐ HEAD LAMP
- ☐ LIGHTER / MATCHES
- ☐ KNIFE / MULTI-TOOL
- ☐ CELL PHONE
- ☐ POUCH
- ☐ MOLESKIN
- ☐ TREKKING POLES

FOOD & SUPPLIES

- ☐ MEALS & SNACKS
- ☐ WATER BOTTLE
- ☐ WATER TREATMENT
- ☐ COOKING POT
- ☐ COOKSTOVE/FUEL
- ☐ EATING UTENSILS
- ☐ BOWL/MUG/PLATE
- ☐ GARBAGE BAGS
- ☐ ROPE
- ☐ FOLDABLE BUCKET

CAMPING GEAR

- ☐ TENT
- ☐ SLEEPING BAG
- ☐ SLEEPING PAD
- ☐ TOILET PAPER
- ☐ BACKPACK
- ☐ DUCT TAPE
- ☐ FOLDING SAW
- ☐ POT LIFTER
- ☐ CAMP SHOES
- ☐ BEAR BANGER

MISC.

- ☐ INSECT REPELLENT
- ☐ LIP BALM
- ☐ FACE PROTECTOR
- ☐ EXTRA GLOVES
- ☐ DEODORANT
- ☐ HEADPHONES
- ☐ BATTERIES
- ☐ CHARGER
- ☐ DECK OF CARDS
- ☐ GPS

OTHER

- ☐ _____
- ☐ _____
- ☐ _____
- ☐ _____
- ☐ _____
- ☐ _____
- ☐ _____
- ☐ _____
- ☐ _____
- ☐ _____

HIKING JOURNAL

TRAIL		ELEVATION GAIN	LOSS
LOCATION			
DISTANCE	DURATION	START TIME	END TIME
TRAIL TYPE	DIFFICULTY	WEATHER	
IMPORTANT TRAIL DETAILS		NOTES	
TRAIL SURFACE	EXPOSURE		

CAMPING *Adventures*

COLOR IN THE DATES WHEN YOU WENT CAMPING

JANUARY

S	M	T	W	T	F	S
		1	2	3	4	5
6	7	8	9	10	11	12
13	14	15	16	17	18	19
20	21	22	23	24	25	26
27	28	29	30	31		

FEBRUARY

S	M	T	W	T	F	S
					1	2
3	4	5	6	7	8	9
10	11	12	13	14	15	16
17	18	19	20	21	22	23
24	25	26	27	28		

MARCH

S	M	T	W	T	F	S
					1	2
3	4	5	6	7	8	9
10	11	12	13	14	15	16
17	18	19	20	21	22	23
24	25	26	27	28	29	30
31						

APRIL

S	M	T	W	T	F	S
	1	2	3	4	5	6
7	8	9	10	11	12	13
14	15	16	17	18	19	20
21	22	23	24	25	26	27
28	29	30				

MAY

S	M	T	W	T	F	S
			1	2	3	4
5	6	7	8	9	10	11
12	13	14	15	16	17	18
19	20	21	22	23	24	25
26	27	28	29	30	31	

JUNE

S	M	T	W	T	F	S
						1
2	3	4	5	6	7	8
9	10	11	12	13	14	15
16	17	18	19	20	21	22
23	24	25	26	27	28	29
30						

JULY

S	M	T	W	T	F	S
	1	2	3	4	5	6
7	8	9	10	11	12	13
14	15	16	17	18	19	20
21	22	23	24	25	26	27
28	29	30	31			

AUGUST

S	M	T	W	T	F	S
				1	2	3
4	5	6	7	8	9	10
11	12	13	14	15	16	17
18	19	20	21	22	23	24
25	26	27	28	29	30	31

SEPTEMBER

S	M	T	W	T	F	S
1	2	3	4	5	6	7
8	9	10	11	12	13	14
15	16	17	18	19	20	21
22	23	24	25	26	27	28
29	30					

OCTOBER

S	M	T	W	T	F	S
		1	2	3	4	5
6	7	8	9	10	11	12
13	14	15	16	17	18	19
20	21	22	23	24	25	26
27	28	29	30	31		

NOVEMBER

S	M	T	W	T	F	S
					1	2
3	4	5	6	7	8	9
10	11	12	13	14	15	16
17	18	19	20	21	22	23
24	25	26	27	28	29	30

DECEMBER

S	M	T	W	T	F	S
1	2	3	4	5	6	7
8	9	10	11	12	13	14
15	16	17	18	19	20	21
22	23	24	25	26	27	28
29	30	31				

CAMPING TRACKER
Where I've Been

CAMPGROUND	LOCATION	DATE

CAMPING RESERVATION

CAMPGROUND PHONE #	RESERVATION DETAILS
CONTACT PERSON	
CAMPGROUND ADDRESS	ACTIVITIES
RESTAURANTS & AMENITIES	NOTES

SITE #	NIGHTLY RATE	CHECK IN	CHECK OUT

CAMPGROUND
Amenities

- WATER
- ELECTRIC
- SEWER
- WIFI
- CABLE TV
- PETS ALLOWED
- FIRE PIT
- SHOWERS
- TENTS PERMITTED
- VISITOR PARKING
- LAUNDRY SERVICES
- BBQ AREA
- SWIMMING
- ACCESS TO BEACH / LAKE
- BOAT LAUNCH
- FISHING

- POOL
- HOT TUB
- ACTIVITY CENTER
- NATURE TRAILS / HIKING
- PLAYGROUND
- BIKING / TRAILS
- GOLF COURSE
- KIDS CENTER
- FIREWORKS
- BINGO
- VOLLEYBALL
- TENNIS COURTS
- GARBAGE DISPOSAL
- CONVENIENCE STORE
- FIREWOOD/KINDLE
- PICNIC TABLES

CAMPING *Shopping List*

CAMPING RESERVATION

CAMPGROUND PHONE #	RESERVATION DETAILS
CONTACT PERSON	
CAMPGROUND ADDRESS	ACTIVITIES
RESTAURANTS & AMENITIES	NOTES

SITE #	NIGHTLY RATE	CHECK IN	CHECK OUT

CAMPGROUND
Amenities

- ◯ WATER
- ◯ ELECTRIC
- ◯ SEWER
- ◯ WIFI
- ◯ CABLE TV
- ◯ PETS ALLOWED
- ◯ FIRE PIT
- ◯ SHOWERS
- ◯ TENTS PERMITTED
- ◯ VISITOR PARKING
- ◯ LAUNDRY SERVICES
- ◯ BBQ AREA
- ◯ SWIMMING
- ◯ ACCESS TO BEACH / LAKE
- ◯ BOAT LAUNCH
- ◯ FISHING
- ◯
- ◯
- ◯

- ◯ POOL
- ◯ HOT TUB
- ◯ ACTIVITY CENTER
- ◯ NATURE TRAILS / HIKING
- ◯ PLAYGROUND
- ◯ BIKING / TRAILS
- ◯ GOLF COURSE
- ◯ KIDS CENTER
- ◯ FIREWORKS
- ◯ BINGO
- ◯ VOLLEYBALL
- ◯ TENNIS COURTS
- ◯ GARBAGE DISPOSAL
- ◯ CONVENIENCE STORE
- ◯ FIREWOOD/KINDLE
- ◯ PICNIC TABLES

CAMPING *Shopping List*

FAMILY CAMPING *Checklist*

IMPORTANT GEAR

- [ ] Tent
- [ ] Backpack
- [ ] Tarp
- [ ] BBQ
- [ ] Sleeping Bag
- [ ] Camping Chairs
- [ ] _____
- [ ] _____
- [ ] _____
- [ ] _____
- [ ] _____

FOOD SUPPLIES

- [ ] Meals
- [ ] Snacks
- [ ] Water & Drinks
- [ ] Cook Set / Pots & Utensils & Dishes
- [ ] Condiments
- [ ] _____
- [ ] _____
- [ ] _____
- [ ] _____
- [ ] _____

CLOTHING

- [ ] Gloves & Hat
- [ ] Hats / Visors
- [ ] Socks & Underwear
- [ ] T-shirts & Sweaters
- [ ] Jacket / Raincoat
- [ ] Hiking Boots
- [ ] _____
- [ ] _____
- [ ] _____
- [ ] _____
- [ ] _____

TOOLS & SUPPLIES

- [ ] Lighter & Flashlights
- [ ] Firewood & Fire Starter
- [ ] Batteries
- [ ] Knife or Multi-Tool
- [ ] Compass
- [ ] _____
- [ ] _____
- [ ] _____
- [ ] _____
- [ ] _____

MISC ITEMS

- [ ] Garbage Bags
- [ ] Sunscreen
- [ ] Bug Spray/ Repellent
- [ ] Towels
- [ ] Water Bottle
- [ ] Toilet Paper
- [ ] _____
- [ ] _____
- [ ] _____
- [ ] _____
- [ ] _____

OTHER

- [ ] _____
- [ ] _____
- [ ] _____
- [ ] _____
- [ ] _____
- [ ] _____
- [ ] _____
- [ ] _____
- [ ] _____
- [ ] _____
- [ ] _____

FAMILY CAMPING *Checklist*

IMPORTANT GEAR

- [ ] _____
- [ ] _____
- [ ] _____
- [ ] _____
- [ ] _____
- [ ] _____
- [ ] _____
- [ ] _____
- [ ] _____
- [ ] _____
- [ ] _____

FOOD SUPPLIES

- [ ] _____
- [ ] _____
- [ ] _____
- [ ] _____
- [ ] _____
- [ ] _____
- [ ] _____
- [ ] _____
- [ ] _____
- [ ] _____
- [ ] _____

CLOTHING

- [ ] _____
- [ ] _____
- [ ] _____
- [ ] _____
- [ ] _____
- [ ] _____
- [ ] _____
- [ ] _____
- [ ] _____
- [ ] _____
- [ ] _____

TOOLS & SUPPLIES

- [ ] _____
- [ ] _____
- [ ] _____
- [ ] _____
- [ ] _____
- [ ] _____
- [ ] _____
- [ ] _____
- [ ] _____
- [ ] _____
- [ ] _____

MISC ITEMS

- [ ] _____
- [ ] _____
- [ ] _____
- [ ] _____
- [ ] _____
- [ ] _____
- [ ] _____
- [ ] _____
- [ ] _____
- [ ] _____
- [ ] _____

OTHER

- [ ] _____
- [ ] _____
- [ ] _____
- [ ] _____
- [ ] _____
- [ ] _____
- [ ] _____
- [ ] _____
- [ ] _____
- [ ] _____
- [ ] _____

CAMPING SUPPLIES

CAMPING Checklist

Shelter
- [ ] TENT / CAMPER
- [ ] SLEEPING BLANKET
- [ ] PILLOWS
- [ ] TARP / COVERING

Comfort
- [ ] SLEEPING BAGS
- [ ] SHEETS & PILLOWS
- [ ] AIR MATTRESS
- [ ] AIR PUMP

Clothing
- [ ] HIKING BOOTS
- [ ] SWEATERS
- [ ] RAIN JACKET
- [ ] WARM SOCKS
- [ ] T-SHIRTS
- [ ] WARM COAT
- [ ] SUN VISOR / HAT
- [ ] BATHING SUIT
- [ ] PYJAMAS

Food
- [ ] FOOD / SUPPLIES
- [ ] CONDIMENTS
- [ ] COOKWARE/POTS
- [ ] TABLE CLOTH
- [ ] PLATES & CUPS
- [ ] UTENSILS
- [ ] PAPER TOWEL
- [ ] POT HOLDERS
- [ ] DISH SOAP
- [ ] CUTLERY

Personal
- [ ] SOAP
- [ ] SHAMPOO
- [ ] TOWELS
- [ ] TOOTHPASTE
- [ ] HAIR BRUSH
- [ ] SUNSCREEN
- [ ] DEODORANT
- [ ] HAND SANITIZER
- [ ] RAZORS

Essentials
- [ ] MEDICATION
- [ ] FIRST AID KIT
- [ ] TOILET PAPER
- [ ] LIP BALM
- [ ] TISSUES
- [ ] MIRROR
- [ ] HAIR CLIPS

Important
- [ ] BATTERIES
- [ ] CAMERA
- [ ] CHARGERS
- [ ] SUNGLASSES
- [ ] FLASHLIGHT
- [ ] BUG SPRAY
- [ ] LANTERNS
- [ ] COMPASS
- [ ] BINOCULARS
- [ ] HIKING GEAR
- [ ] BACKPACK

CAMPING *Checklist*

Entertainment

- [ ] BOARD GAMES
- [ ] CARDS
- [ ] RADIO
- [ ] SPORTS GEAR

Cleaning

- [ ] BROOM / MOP
- [ ] CLEANING SUPPLIES
- [ ] CLEANING CLOTHS
- [ ] DISH TOWELS

Misc

- [ ] COFFEE POT
- [ ] FIRE KETTLE
- [ ] COOLER & ICE
- [ ] FOLDABLE TABLE
- [ ] CAMPING CHAIRS
- [ ] LIGHTER / FUEL
- [ ] FIREWOOD
- [ ] BBQ GRLL
- [ ] GARBAGE BAGS

Shopping List

CAMPING MEAL
Planner

MONDAY	TUESDAY

WEDNESDAY	THURSDAY

FRIDAY	SATURDAY

SUNDAY	SNACK IDEAS

CAMPING *Activities*

Monday

Tuesday

Wednesday

Thursday

Friday

Saturday

Sunday

MY CAMPING *Journal*

DATE:

WHAT I DID TODAY

HIGHLIGHT OF THE DAY

www.ingramcontent.com/pod-product-compliance
Lightning Source LLC
Chambersburg PA
CBHW080215040426
42333CB00044B/2682